RELATIONSHIP AFTER CHEATING

A GUIDE TO RECOVERY FROM INFIDELITY, REBUILDING TRUST AND MOVING FORWARD

ELLIE K. FLORES

SEVEN SUNS BOOK PRESS

CONTENTS

BONUS BOOK

How to Discover and Confront Infidelity in Your Relationship

Unravels the many warning signs a cheating partner displays, and discovers how to confirm those suspicions, and confronts them with evidence.

(Download at www.littlebookhut.com)

INTRODUCTION

NOTHING BREAKS A HEART more than when your partner has an affair. An extramarital affair, for many couples, means the end of the relationship. But some come out of it stronger than ever. Their chemistry, communication, and connection increase. It's like they start to see themselves for the very first time. But this affection and acceptance don't come easy.

Whether to stay and work on the marriage or leave the cheating partner... a question that has challenged the foundations of even the strongest of loves.

Infidelity—a word as obnoxious as the act itself. Many call it the ultimate relationship killer, a no-go area, and a direct violation of an otherwise beautiful relationship. For centuries, researchers have tried to understand the psychology behind an act of cheating, and come to conclude that it is rarely as simple as having an intimate affair with another person. There are layers and layers of why men and women cheat, especially when they are bound in the sacred relationship we call marriage.

Additionally, do men and women cheat for different reasons or the same? What is the motivation behind infidelity? What goes on in one's mind before one commits adultery? Is one blinded by pure lust, or is there something deeper at work?

Having studied human behavior, especially in matters of love and commitment, I truly believe that every relationship, no matter how rocky, has a chance of survival. But this survival depends on how the cheater and cheated spouse take things forward. The whole notion behind why one cheats, what happens when they get caught, and how they move from there, is quite fascinating. It has intrigued me for years, so most of my research has been dedicated to understanding how some people remain committed to their partners all their lives, while some cheat on them despite having everything they could have wished for.

It is difficult to define cheating today as new approaches to dating and courtship are introduced. When we were young, we didn't have apps like Tinder or Bumble to connect with partners. We had to go down the proper route of dating. Now, however, with open and non-monogamous relationships, easy access to social media sites, pornography, and different mental and emotional needs, every relationship dynamic becomes complex.

Some couples are okay with their partner spending too much time watching pornography, while others raise eyebrows over a liked photo on Instagram, or a snap sent to an ex or stranger. What transpires, though, is that every attempt at cheating has some secrecy and guilt attached to it. The cheater wants to keep it a secret because they don't want to get caught. Also, if the cheater feels guilty about it while doing it, it means they know it isn't appropriate or acceptable behavior.

There are several types of affairs, but the core remains the same. Whether it is forgivable or not depends on the couple entirely. Will they survive this shock together, or go their separate ways? Will they remain in an unhappy marriage for the sake of the kids, or leave and marry someone else?

The reason for writing this book is to help you understand the reasons that lead to one spouse cheating on the other, identify them, and find ways to resolve them.

Not every marriage is salvageable, but if you think yours is, how will you overcome what you feel right now about what happened? Do you find initiating physical relationships with your cheating partner something you can do? If so, how? How can you rebuild trust? How can you mend your broken heart?

Most importantly, how can you recover from infidelity?

Let's explore all such queries and much more in this brief guide, and address the aftermath of what happens between couples when a partner is caught cheating, or confesses to cheating after feeling guilty.

Starting with what counts as cheating, let's categorize types of affairs to understand why people cheat.

IS CHEATING ALWAYS SEXUAL?

MOST AFFAIRS ARE LABELED as romantic or sexual affairs. They don't just happen like a one-night stand or accidental affair. They may take weeks or months to build and prosper before both partners decide to act on their feelings and get intimate. Since the feelings are so strong, acting on them doesn't feel wrong, at least not at the moment.

But romantic affairs aren't the only type of affairs. Accidental affairs or one-night stands are another common type of affair people have. They happen in the heat of the moment, under the assumption that people can get away with them without repercussions, or when they are under the influence of alcohol or drugs. These are events of opportunity and convenience. There isn't any emotional attachment though. Business trips, for example, provide the perfect setting for a one-night stand. Most spouses who engage in one-night stands stay in their marriages, but have feelings of guilt or fear.

Emotional affairs are another form of affair people have. According to Truth About Deception, a community that conducts surveys and online quizzes, 90% of women and 77% of men who took part in the surveys admitted to having an emotional affair (Cheating Spouse Survey Results—Truth about Deception, n.d.).

Emotional affairs are often platonic and nonsexual. They usually start off as friendship with a coworker, neighbor, another kid's parent, or a child's teacher. Eventually, this friendship morphs into something deeper and emotionally intimate. You feel comfortable sharing intimate details about yourself and your life with this person. You offload your problems on them. You feel more recognized, seen, and appreciated when with them.

Digital affairs weren't an invention of the past. You can't blame boomers for it. It is the weapon of today's millennials. Around 40% of women and 30% of men admit to having used social media sites to have an affair. People can be whoever they want to be, have an online persona different from who they are, and disguise their true selves behind filters of all sorts. Steamy chat room conversations, text messages, and DMs have triggered a new form of infidelity. An affair becomes troublesome when you start having conversations you should be having with your spouse with someone else. You talk about experiences, emotions, feelings, and everything else that seems relevant or important to you. Since you can type, backspace, and delete evidence in seconds, there is little guilty conscience.

Add to that apps that facilitates dating and sex like Tinder, Bumble, OkCupid, etc. It's easy to make a profile without any background checks, and access potential partners in your area. What more can you wish for?

But why do men and women cheat, what causes them to cheat, and what do they seek from an affair? Let's dive right into that first!

INFIDELITY IN MODERN TIMES

Cheating is a personal decision. Some people
will never cheat no matter how bad it is;
others will cheat no matter how good it is!

– Dr. Farrah Gray

CHEATING IN MODERN TIMES is different than it was
in the past. Like family dynamics, marriages too, have
changed in the 21st century. So have the rates of infidelity.
Earlier, you could only have an affair with someone in your
town, at least 99% of the time. Today, with technology
and the internet, you can have an emotional affair with
someone from across the globe. All types of infidelity

have become common, as it's easier to meet, connect, and interact with strangers. Did you know there are even websites that promote infidelity and extramarital affairs? They proudly proclaim that they allow men and women an outlet to deal with frustration in their marriages by connecting with other people, and preserve more marriages than they break up. They claim to give unhappy spouses who are heading for a divorce a means to release their frustrations elsewhere, and still be in the marriage.

Sounds contradictory but true; at least that's what the site is all about. And there isn't just one. There are several. But whatever it is, you can't deny the hurt and disgust you feel when you find out you have been cheated by someone who meant the world to you. Nothing can be more humiliating than to know that the person you gave everything to didn't care, and wanted more.

Besides, marriage is based on loyalty and honesty. It is based on mutual respect and affection. Remove all that from the equation, and we are left with nothing.

The social networking boom since the 21st century has also made it easier to rekindle an old spark or find a lost love. There are numerous stories about how two people who had been high school sweethearts reconnected and fell in love again. The odd thing is that when we do that, we forget how bad and toxic that relationship had been. In fact, we glorify it by mentally editing out the wrongs and comparing them with our current married lives. Surely that freedom and casualness can't be expected today when you have been married for more than a decade. However, with sites like Facebook, that lost love is just a search away.

But infidelity isn't something new. It's just how it is becoming acceptable, common, and easy. With more and more couples opting for open marriages, the definition of cheating changes. It is easier to deceive, tell lies, keep secrets, and betray your spouse without thinking about the consequences.

But what do modern men and women seek from an affair? What are they after that they aren't getting from their existing spouse?

MEN VS. WOMEN: WHAT REASONS PERSUADE THEM

RESEARCHERS SET OUT TO seek answers as to why men and women cheat despite being committed. Emerging adults were questioned about their experiences with infidelity and closeness with their current partners. Three-fourths cited the need for interdependence as the chief reason for cheating, meaning they weren't getting what they wanted from their current partners or relationship. The cheating allowed them to seek it from some place else, a place far more exciting.

The second most common reason was the need for some freedom and independence from their partners to seek out their own identity.

The study, although small-scale, did provide some insights into how modern-day people view relationships and why they cheat. As they aren't big on traditions, they would rather hang out with their friends, move in with their partners, and go about their lives without having the need to sign a marriage contract. With no binding contract, the idea of cheating becomes more approachable. Since so many of them are doing it, cheating becomes somewhat acceptable and forgivable. They don't view infidelity as problematic.

But for those who are in a binding contract, what motivates them to cheat?

Frustrations in marriage, and lack of appreciation and validation are the biggest reasons why partners grow apart, and rely on others to find that joy they thought their marriage would bring. Couples today would agree to go to a marriage counselor, but not talk themselves. They would rather have a third person come in and resolve their issues than communicate and resolve them themselves.

Sometimes people carry so much emotional baggage in the form of neglect, abusive or toxic parents, or some childhood trauma that they can't sustain a committed relationship. Adults who have grown up seeing their parents argue and fight all the time are more likely to expect the same from their relationship. Deep down, they feel that their relationship too will suffer a dip down the line and will become the same. This preconceived notion in their head makes it easier for them to cheat, because they already know how it is all going to end.

Then there is unhappiness and dissatisfaction in marriages. Sexual or emotional incompatibility can also make partners commit infidelity. Do you think this could have been the reason why your partner cheated on you? Do you feel they were unhappy or dissatisfied in the marriage?

Long-distance relationships also provide some grounds for disloyalty to many couples. They see it as an opportunity to have a fling, or to have their needs met by someone else when their partner isn't there for them.

Boredom could also be one of the factors. Love takes effort. Expecting your partner to love you like the day when you got married is delusional, especially when you aren't making the effort to keep the spark alive. If your partner sees that you have stopped making the effort to dress up, take them on a date, surprise them with a gift, or simply keep the romance alive, they might seek it from elsewhere.

Another common reason is aging and body issues. When men and women pass their primes and don't see themselves as attractive anymore, anyone that comes along and reminds them that they have still got it becomes a favorite. Who wouldn't want to be reminded that they are sexy, handsome, or hot every day? Would you not fall for the person who tells you this?

Revenge sex may also be the reason. When one partner cheats, the other will cheat on them as revenge to get back and even the score. This is problematic in all ways as the goal is to hurt each other and nothing more. Poor boundaries may also determine cheating. When both partners aren't clear on what counts as cheating and what doesn't, one or both of them are bound to find themselves in trouble over trivial things. For example, your partner may just be a sweet talker. Their intention may not be to flirt with the opposite sex. However, you might see it as unacceptable because you don't want your partner to speak or engage in any casual talk with the opposite gender. However, if you didn't communicate this to your partner earlier, you can't expect them to know. Be clear from the start and if your partner still continues with the charade, then it's a problem.

The reason your spouse used to cheat tells you a lot about whether the act is forgivable or not. Cheating may be a one-time offense for a spouse. They may have done it when not in their best state. Does that mean they should have a chance at forgiveness?

What makes a relationship salvageable, and what makes it null and void? What factors should come into play, given that you have to make the choice either to stay or leave? Are those factors worth your self-respect? Are they important enough to make you reconsider leaving and, instead, stay and work on your marriage?

These are some important questions you must think about if you have just found out about your spouse's unfaithfulness. Let's examine these and make the right choice.

DECISIONS, DECISIONS, DECISIONS... SALVAGE IT OR LET GO?

Marriage stands the test of times when both you and your spouse work towards making things better. And we are tested the most when we face adversities. If you can sail through the adversities as one, as a team, then you have won half the battle.

– Unknown

WHEN A PARTNER CHEATS, the main tenet of a healthy relationship—trust—leaves. Its value shatters. For most couples, the hardest challenge is regaining that lost trust. How can you trust someone who broke the vow of your marriage to remain loyal, love, and appreciate? But as easy as it seems, marriage counselors report that most of the couples who face infidelity reconcile and get back together after some time. They decide to stay together based on a number of reasons.

Sometimes, they put their grievances behind them because they have kids who are growing into amazing adults. They don't want to trouble them, or cause them any problems with the separation. Some couples can't bear the cost of raising kids alone, or don't have the financial means to do so. They are already struggling to keep things afloat, and separation would only make matters worse. At other times, some couples know how much the cheating partner loves their children and don't have the heart to pull them apart.

But each couple and their situation is unique. You can't expect a one-size-fits-all approach here. If your partner has cheated on you, there are many things to consider. The emotions you are going through right now may cloud your judgment. You are angry, hurt, and emotional. You had only heard about it happening to other couples and pitied them. But now it has hit home, and you don't know how to deal with it.

A thousand thoughts are going through your mind. Should you leave or stay? What if you leave? What if you stay? Should you ask others, or go with what your gut tells you?

Let me make it slightly, if not completely, easier for you. After some thorough understanding and research, I have compiled a list of questions that you must answer to know what your heart truly desires. But before you answer them, let me tell you something. Your answers will change as your heart starts to heal. You will overcome the emotional mess you are in right now after a couple of weeks. So don't answer these questions just once. Answer these every other week to see if your answers change or remain the same.

- Is it a pattern or is this the first time it has happened? Did they cheat on someone else to be with you? Or is it something that happened out of the blue?

- After cheating, has your spouse shifted toward honesty, or are they still covering up and lying? Do they still make up stories about why it happened or how it happened? Are their stories never consistent when you ask them where they were or what they were doing? Or have they been honest and remorseful after that one episode?

- Is there genuine remorse in their behavior, or are they sorry solely because they got caught? If it's the first, consider staying and working things through.

- Have they accepted responsibility for it, or are they still making excuses or putting the blame on you, alcohol, or some stress from work? Ideally, your partner must take full responsibility for cheating, whether they committed it intentionally or on impulse.

- What reasons did your spouse give for cheating on you? Do you believe them and why? If the reason is absurd and careless, is it worth putting in the effort?

- Did your spouse truly apologize for their behavior or just called it a mistake and asked for forgiveness and consideration? If they called it just a mistake, make sure they are ready to pay for it by staying loyal to you forever.

- Can they guarantee it won't happen in the future again? What guarantees can they offer, and how true do you think they are? Do you think they have it in them to remain loyal this time?

- Is your spouse a good person and has done something bad? Can you separate your partner from their actions? Do you think they are truly miserable about what happened? If you can see them as separate from their act, and know that they are a good person, then consider seeing a counselor and staying.

- Are they eager to earn back your trust and make the relationship work, or have they given up on it already and left the decision with you? Any partner who is truly sorry about their actions will try to win you back at any cost. Is your partner making any such efforts to rebuild trust?

- Are you considering staying together for yourself or for the sake of your kids or family? Are you in it with all your heart, or do you still think you need more time to think things through? Ideally, you should put yourself first.

- Does your spouse expect you to get over it as soon as possible, or do they allow you to have as much time as you need? They shouldn't dictate how long you need to heal.

- Was your relationship at a standstill when your spouse cheated? Were you together, separated, or fighting all the time? Was your marriage on the verge of divorce already, or were you blissfully happy and never noticed a thing out of the ordinary in your partner?

- Does your partner understand the consequences of their actions? Do they know the amount of hurt they have caused you? Are they willing to change and accept your terms if you decide to get back together and work on your marriage?

- Has your spouse severed all ties with the one they cheated on you with, or are they still connected? If your spouse works with them, how do they plan to maintain distance?

- How open is your partner to the idea of marital and individual counseling? Do they think it is something you two need to get over together, or are they willing to see someone about it?

- Can you trust your partner again? Do you believe the relationship is worth saving? Do you think you can again be as happy and joyous as you were before?

- Or do you think their unfaithfulness will forever haunt you? Do you think you will never find it in your heart to forgive them? Are you considering retaliation or revenge?

Answering these questions with a clear head and open heart will tell you what you need to do next. Keep asking yourself these questions time and time again, and see how your answers change with time.

Once you have answered all the questions, you will have three choices:

1. Leave now.

2. Give your heart some time to heal before making hasty decisions.

3. Stay on.

I Am Still Unsure... What To Do?

BEFORE YOU GO ASKING me or anyone else around you, remember that this is a decision only you can take. It isn't your family that your spouse betrayed. It isn't their trust that they broke. It is yours. Are you willing to look past it all and move forward? Do you think you have it within you to forgive them? Your family will obviously take your side and tell you to leave your partner. But if you still love them and know that they are a better person than that, reconsider.

Talk about how much hurt they have caused so they understand the damage they have done. Let it all out once and for all. Shout, curse, and fight. Don't let anything remain inside, or else it will come back to haunt you in case you decide to stay and work on your marriage. Once you feel relieved and unburdened, talk about how you are going to resolve the underlying issues that caused your partner to seek love elsewhere. Talk about the reasons that triggered the need. Could it be your negligence or lack of interest?

Once you understand the reasons behind their actions, you can better make up your mind about what decision to make. You can also go to therapy and seek professional counseling. This will allow you to know how you can rebuild trust, start afresh, and avoid any recurrences of such acts.

But first, allow yourself some time to heal. If seeing your partner in front of you is something your heart can't take, go to a friend's or relative's house. Take as much time as you need to get past your grief. Your heart has been wounded. Your capacity to think clearly may be disabled. You may have mixed feelings about what you are feeling. Hurt may show off as anger. Sadness may take the shape of irritability. Pain may manifest in weird ways. So let your heart heal. Let it feel at peace again. Cry if you feel like crying. Let those emotions out so that when you do feel ready to make a choice, you make the right one.

If you decide to forgive your spouse, you have to do it wholeheartedly. This isn't the kind of argument that you can bring up over and over again during fights. This isn't something you will have to hold against them later, because it was up to you to make the call. Stay only if you think you can move past this trauma. Stay only if you feel ready to reconcile with your spouse. Stay only if you trust them again with your delicate heart. If you make the choice to stay, you and your partner will have to do some real work. Communication will be the essence of it as you move past your current state.

Let's learn how things will work out and change between the two of you.

WHAT HAPPENS IF I STAY?

And suddenly you just know it's time to start something new and trust the magic's beginning.

– Mandy Hale

THE DECISION TO STAY or leave isn't something you can take in a heartbeat. You already know of the many factors to consider before reaching a conclusion. But let's assume that you do decide to stay. What's next? Will forgiveness come easily? What expectations will you have from your partner now that the dynamics of your relationship have changed? Before we delve into that, let's quickly revisit the most common reasons why partners cheat on their spouses.

We shall address each reason one by one, providing suggestions as to how you can move past what has happened and, hopefully, prevent it from happening again.

Reason #1: Lack of Emotional Intimacy

Lack of intimacy between partners is the #1 reason for cheating among married couples. Life gets hard. It doesn't remain the same as those honeymooning days. Stress at work, child-rearing, chores, and building a career all happen at once. What little time there was for romance goes after taking care of children and fulfilling their needs. Partners begin to miss their carefree days. They begin to miss each other. They miss talking on the phone, going on dates, or having those sexual urges. They miss all the fun they had when life was simpler and more romantic. This distance furthers their emotional intimacy too. Couples feel they are no longer as connected as they were before. Communication becomes limited to what expectations one has from the other in terms of responsibilities like taking the kids to school, paying the bills, or grocery shopping.

Now enters a stranger who is either single or dealing with similar issues in their marriage. A single individual reminds the married partner what they are missing out on. A married stranger battling the same conflicts finds an instant emotional connection. Suddenly, the cheating partner finds someone with whom they can open up about their worries. The more conversations they have, the more similarities they find in their lives. The more similarities, the stronger their emotional bond. They both start seeking the same thing—love and respect. When two people feel connected, the odds of acting on the temptations that arise in their minds grow stronger. But emotional intimacy doesn't always lead to a sexual encounter. It may as well be between people of the same sex. So sexual intimacy isn't always the main concern.

But a problem arises when the cheating partner becomes distant from their married partner and neglects them. That's when the actual cheating happens. It doesn't happen behind closed doors, but rather in the minds of those two cheating partners.

If this has been the case with your marriage, then you need to work on rebuilding emotional intimacy with your partner. You have to give them time, listen to what they say, and be present both emotionally and physically.

What Partners Need to Do

Restoring emotional intimacy in relationships that have suffered infidelity is difficult, but not impossible. With some counseling and therapy, partners can once again feel affectionate and connected to each other, given that they understand what they must do. The following describes what they need to do.

Find out what type of affection they seek. Are they more verbal in their affection, or would they want a tangible gift to know they are loved? We all have different ways we like to be wowed by our partners. You may seek verbal affection and appreciation while your partner feels more connected when they receive something valuable as a present. To revive emotional intimacy after infidelity, both partners should reassess how they like to be wowed. Hence, they know what to expect from their partner and what expectations their partner has.

Second, find things that you both enjoy doing together. It could be taking a trip, watching a favorite show together, or cooking. To ensure that an emotional connection has been reestablished, couples must spend quality time together. Set aside some time every night to be with each other. Leave your phones behind, and do something you both enjoy. Talk about how your day went, what you plan to do tomorrow, and make plans for the weekend. Plan dates and fun nights where you let go of yourself a little, and enjoy each other's company to the fullest.

Identify why you feel disconnected from your spouse. For emotional intimacy to foster, it is important to address the issues that concern you. Talk to your partner about your worries. Do you think your lack of closeness is because you are having a hard time trusting your partner? Is it because you have poor self-esteem? Identifying why you feel distant from your spouse can, again, give you a chance to work on those problems and start afresh.

Don't let issues fester. Address them as they arise. Couples that harbor resentment toward their partners ruin emotional intimacy. Speak up when something bothers you. Don't keep it in and think that you can solve it on your own. Get their attention by saying things like:

- Could you please lend me a minute and hear me out?

- There is something bothering me and I don't want to sleep without discussing it.

- I didn't like the way you joked about me in front of your family. Can you be a bit considerate the next time?

Be vulnerable together. Vulnerability is the ability to express openly how you feel. If your partner's actions, words, or behaviors hurt you, voice your concerns. Patiently, remind them how their rudeness affects your mood and causes pain. Having open communication about how you two feel about each other will help you rebuild trust in one another and restore emotional intimacy.

Reason #2: Lack of Sexual Compatibility

A few years down the lane, couples begin to get lazy about sex. What was once the driving force of their marriage takes a back seat as other things get in the front. Kids, increased financial responsibilities, bills, mortgage, work stress, and social media leaves couples with little time to spend with one another. Whether you were married yesterday or a decade ago, sexual compatibility between partners is imperative. Today, most couples who have been together a year or more become complacent about their sexual lives.

In a marriage, when partners have mismatched libidos, a vicious cycle of pursuer-distancer begins. A spouse with a higher sex drive becomes the pursuer, always chasing after the less-interested partner for sexual intimacy. Repeated rejection by the distancer becomes frustrating, causing anger and pain. This leads to fights and arguments between them.

Suddenly, the partner with the lower sex drive becomes the culprit. They become the ones always coming up with excuses to avoid intimacy. They are reluctant to kiss or hug their spouse because they know what it would eventually lead to. When issues with mismatched libidos remain unaddressed, the pursuer seeks physical intimacy from outside, whereas the distancer looks to connect with someone emotionally.

What Partners Need to Do

This is why conversations around sexual compatibility are important. Expecting either partner to sacrifice isn't fair. Unless there is a compromise in place, both partners will likely look for an emotional and physical connection from someplace else. Partners with high libidos may develop poor self-esteem when they are frequently rejected. They may build resentment toward their partners. Partners with low libidos may feel guilty, pressured, or ashamed about not being able to meet their partner's demands. So, how do you prevent that from happening? Here's how.

Mix things up a little. Share fantasies and fetishes. Dress up and role-play. Don't come off too strong or be lazy about sex. Denying your partner's sexual needs won't stop them from fulfilling them. They will only stop fulfilling them with you.

Initiate sex more often. Gone are those days when men were the only ones initiating physical intimacy. Be forthcoming when you feel like it. Chase your partner like you would like to be chased.

Excite your partner with some casual teasing. Send a sexy photo of you reminding them what awaits them. Share memes about sex. Bookmark unique sexual positions to try the next time you have sex. Do it in locations other than your bedroom. Our brains experience more pleasure when there is the anticipation of a reward. Let that pleasure reach its peak before the reward is shared.

Don't bring to bed discussions about your kid's teachers or household chores. Let your bedroom be a place for pleasure. Sexual arousal declines when the mind is distracted or stressed out.

Don't make sex the only time you two are together. Add to your daily routine some hugs, cuddles, and kisses. Give your partner a foot massage while watching TV, rub your partner's shoulders before sleeping, and take a bath together. Focus on making every touch affectionate and passionate.

To prevent mismatched libidos from ruining your intimacy, talk about what excites your partner. Maybe it is how you touch them that displeases them. Reach a compromise if the needs of both partners can't be met. Make sure you both are aware of what it means for your relationship.

Reason #3: Issues Related to Self-Esteem

Your self-esteem plays a huge role in how you relate to others. From an early age, we have been taught to seek approval for everything we do. We asked our parents for guidance and mentorship. Then we relied on our teachers to instill some knowledge, discipline, and manners. Our friends helped shape our personalities. We asked for their opinions on everything. Then, we fell in love and got married. The need for validation and approval remained the same. We wanted our partners to appreciate and value us. We wanted them to feel like they had won the lottery by being with us. In the beginning, your partner did by doing all the things that guaranteed their interest and affection. But then they stopped. You began to question everything. Do they still like me? Do they find me attractive, or are they ashamed of me?

This insecurity in relationships, especially between married people, causes partners to cheat on each other.

Our self-esteem gets crippled as our partners stop valuing us as they did before. And sometimes you also let yourself go, not realizing that your partner expects you to look your best and maintain your good looks and weight.

However, when this validation begins to come from elsewhere, say from a colleague, boss, or friend, you feel alive again. When you get compliments from people other than your spouse, infidelity becomes exciting. You start getting validation from someone other than your partner, and let's be honest, it feels good.

Cheating becomes an emotional outlet where you relive your days of freedom and carelessness. It becomes an escape from your married life and insecurities. It gives you an instant self-esteem boost when you know someone has the hots for you.

You may also experience low self-esteem when you see other couples your age living their best lives. They are going on vacations, planning their third or fourth honeymoons, while you remain stuck in a boring marriage.

What Partners Need to Do

Partners should always be the biggest cheerleaders for their significant other. They should be the ones who stand beside them in both good and bad times. Self-esteem issues that arise in marriages arise because one or both partners feels unwanted and unloved. If you think your partner suffers from low self-esteem, make sure that they overcome those feelings with some help from you. How can you help them? Here's how.

Focus on their strengths. It's easy to point out the negative qualities in someone and overlook their positives. When couples share a house together, they often come across qualities they don't like in their spouses. However, it's one thing to ask them to change, and another to nag and berate them about it. If the goal is to help your partner overcome their low self-esteem, be sure to point out what makes them perfect. Focus on what they do right, and compliment and ignore the things they do wrong.

Second, identify the areas where they feel insecure. Sometimes we keep telling ourselves pessimistic stories. It's time you help your partner reframe those negative thoughts that make them feel insecure about themselves and help them overcome those challenges. For example, if your partner feels insecure about their weight, look up some gyms in your area and sign them up. You can also partner up with them and help them reach their desired weight goals.

Validate your partner's feelings about themselves instead of telling them to get over them. The way we think about ourselves usually stems from something deeper within us. Maybe your partner thinks you are too good to be with them. Maybe they think you deserve someone better than them. Validating your partner's feelings will help them express themselves more confidently. More importantly, they will stop seeking that validation and approval from elsewhere.

Let them know verbally and nonverbally how proud you are of them. No matter how small or big their success, show enthusiasm for it. Give them credit abundantly, especially when you are in the company of others. Celebrate their wins, so they can feel appreciated.

Don't hold back on how you feel about them. Many times, partners assume that their partners know how they feel about them. It doesn't matter if you live under the same roof, share a bed, or spend most of your days together. Love requires verbal and nonverbal appreciation and affection. Pay attention to the small things your partner does. For example, if they are dressed for an event, compliment them on how beautiful they look, how brilliantly the color complements their skin tone, and how good they smell.

Reason #4: Feeling Unappreciated

Sometimes, one of the partners feels unappreciated for all that they do. They want their partners to help and contribute to the house, and look after the kids. But they fail to communicate this need directly, and wish that their partner would miraculously understand. The deprived partner then becomes more and more resentful toward their partner, expecting more attention, respect, and love. When they don't receive it from their spouse, they start to look for those things from strangers.

This happens most commonly when both partners have unrealistic expectations from one another. How would you feel about your partner not paying attention to you, neglecting you, and not taking care of your needs? Hurtful, right? But what if I tell you that the other partner feels the same? They look after the kids all day, help them with their homework, cook for them, and clean the house, expecting you to appreciate, if not contribute. But you assume they are neglecting you when in reality, they have too much to do on their own.

This lack of clear communication can make both partners feel annoyed at each other. They both may look for companionship and appreciation from people other than their spouses.

What Partners Need to Do

Every human deserves respect, affection, and recognition. You wouldn't work in an office under an ungrateful boss. Then why expect your partner to remain loyal and "at your bidding" when you don't appreciate them for all they put up with? Sounds a bit unfair, no? So, what can you do?

Say things like "thank you" and "I love you" more often. Appreciate the little things your partner does, even as small as handing you the towel when you ask for it from the bathroom, or opening the car door for you. Say thank you when they open a jar's cap for you, or when they find your wallet from under the pillow. Words of kindness and appreciation can improve emotional intimacy too, as both partners then feel loved.

Make a list of some nice things you would want your partner to do for you and ask them to make a similar list. Then, attempt one thing every day to ensure that you and your partner feel appreciated. The list can include ideas like:

- I would love to go on a spontaneous date.

- I would appreciate it if you would help me with laundry and cleaning around the house.

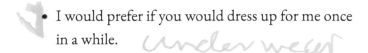

- I would prefer if you would dress up for me once in a while. *underwear*

Give your partner your undivided attention. Set aside some time to spend with just the two of you. Don't talk about the kids or work. Just talk about yourselves and how you are feeling. Share your goals and dreams. Make a bucket list of places you wish to travel to.

Support each other no matter what. Nothing butchers a relationship faster than criticism and negativity from your partner. Complement each other in front of your respective friends and family. Have their back at all times. Stand up for them when someone puts them down. Your partner should know they can always count on you for everything.

I guess I did

Why "My" Partner Cheated

Here's the interesting part. Many marriages face more than one of these issues. Lack of sexual intimacy also means poor emotional connection. If you aren't getting sexually intimate with your spouse, you can lose the emotional connection too. Every sexual connection requires some form of emotional connection. Without that, it's just physical.

Similarly, one partner may have a higher libido and be repeatedly rejected by the other. This will affect the way they feel about themselves. If my partner doesn't want to get intimate with me, there must be something wrong with me, right? That's the first thought that will cross your mind.

The same is the case when there is neglect and a lack of appreciation. Your spouse may feel unappreciated, and thus not want to engage in any sexual intimacy with you. Or you may feel like they are always pressuring you into having sex with them without wanting to connect with you emotionally.

The point is that if a spouse has cheated; find out what made them do it. If it isn't like them, what compelled them to take that step? Could you have contributed to their infidelity? Could it be your neglect and lack of appreciation that made your spouse want to go after someone else? Or do you think it was their high libido that they needed to satisfy?

What caused the episode(s) of cheating? Think about it and think about it non-judgementally. Of course, there is no doubt that their actions have hurt you to your core. Of course, there is no denying that they should be forgiven right away.

The reason I want you to focus more on the problem rather than the person is so that you can figure out how you wish to address it.

- Was it a lack of sexual or emotional intimacy? How will you overcome it?

- Was it neglect and lack of appreciation? How will you mend ties and make things great again?

- Were mismatched libidos to blame? How can you reach a compromise where neither of you feel they should have to give in?

Moreover, you both need to put in the work, not just the one who cheated. Surely, they will have to do more, but you can't take the back seat either. It is easier to blame them for their actions but not look at what triggered those. If you had any part to play in it, if you were inconsistent with your love or distant with your spouse pre-cheating, then you need to make amends too.

But for now, I want to discuss what happens when partners decide to stay together. What happens when, after infidelity, they work together to rebuild trust? Moreover, what can you, as the betrayed, expect to go through during the recovery stage?

INFIDELITY RECOVERY —
WHAT'S NEXT?

Cry. Forgive. Learn. Move on. Let your tears water the seeds of your future happiness.

– Steve Maraboli

THE PAIN, THE ANGUISH you feel is still hard to describe. You want to escape it. You want to curl up in bed, under the covers, and cry your heart out. You wish you wouldn't see the image of your spouse cheating on you with someone whenever you close your eyes. You just want it all to be a nightmare you could wake up from.

Many relationships, as per marriage coaches and counselors, grow stronger after surviving infidelity. This won't happen right away, but after both partners have taken the time to address the concerns they have and decided to move forward, leaving their past behind. This requires that both spouses are dedicated to forgiving each other and healing.

The goal of any cheating recovery stage is to find a way to forgive one another. If your partner cheated on you, it doesn't mean that only they seek forgiveness. It could have been your actions or behavior that made them do it. So you must be willing to change your ways too.

But right now, the pain is unbearable. You wonder if you will ever feel normal again. You wonder if you will ever overcome this trauma and go on with your life as before, with your partner beside you. But how can you be with them when you can't even look them in the eye? Sure, they are sorry, but that does nothing to your wounded heart, does it?

The process of recovery will be difficult. You will go through several stages that will make you wonder if you have it within you to forgive your spouse and reconcile. Let me take you through each stage briefly to normalize everything you are going through. You may already be in the second stage and not know about it, or you haven't even gathered the courage to begin.

What To Expect During and After Infidelity Recovery Stages

Before you begin, understand that there isn't a timeline that you need to follow. Depending on how hurt you are, how long you have been with your partner, what sacrifices you have made in the marriage, and what made you decide to stay rather than leave, you may need more time than others to cope during this difficult time.

Healing begins when you identify the reasons why something happened. What made your partner hurt you most awfully? Why couldn't they have just called it quits? Why did they feel the need to seek companionship outside of their marriage? If there were concerns, why didn't they put them forth?

The first stage of the infidelity recovery stage is the discovery stage. During this stage, you have just come to terms with what has happened, not why it has happened. This is the phase of the initial shock and emotional instability. Your whole world has come crumbling down. You try to make sense of what has happened. If your partner has made the dreadful confession themselves, this is also the time for apologies. Your partner will cry, beg, and feel guilty for having caused you this pain.

The first stage of discovery is followed by unspeakable anger. You feel enraged at your partner and the intruder that broke you two apart. You may also experience self-doubt, lowered self-esteem, and other negative emotions. Ideally, this stage should take as long as six weeks. If you think you need longer than six weeks to come to terms with it, reestablishing trust may become difficult.

The second stage is the grief stage. Grief comes interlaced with many difficult emotions. You will find yourself reliving your life before the affair. You will reminisce about how happy you were with your partner during the initial years of dating and marriage. Grief is an essential stage of healing. Unless you allow yourself to fully mourn the betrayal, you will never recover completely. Many people never fully pass this stage. They remain fixated on how their life was. They question everything about their life with their spouse. Allow yourself to grieve. You may have support from your cheating partner, but it is you who has to recover, not them. Take care of your needs. Put yourself first. Cry, scream, and then cry some more. Work through the sadness, one day at a time. Seek therapy if needed. Ask for support from friends and family. Once you come to terms with your tragedy, you can move toward the next stage, called acceptance.

By this time, you have already decided whether to stay or leave your cheating partner. You have grieved the death of your love. If you decide to leave, there is little that will stop you. If you decide to stay, most of the work will be done during this stage. In the acceptance stage, couples start to talk about what happened and why it happened more openly. It doesn't hurt as much as it did initially, which is why partners can communicate their concerns and listen better. A shared understanding of what reasons made your partner commit cheating happens. You accept that it happened to you, and begin to forgive your partner. It may take months or even a year to be fully able to trust them again with your heart. During this stage, you start to see your partner apart from their actions. You make peace with what happened.

The final stage is the reconciliation stage. Couples who decide to work on their relationship move toward reconnecting. If they have been living apart, they will come to live together and start afresh. Unlike before, they will try to be more expressive of their feelings and emotions. They won't keep secrets and be open about their needs and expectations from one another. This reconnection isn't only with your partner; you also need to reconnect with yourself. You need to reconnect with who you were before the affair happened. You need to reconnect with your idea of being in love. You need to reconnect with what expectations you had from your partner, etc

REBUILDING TRUST— MAKING IT BETTER THAN BEFORE

INFIDELITY MAY LEAVE THE partner being cheated on and feeling betrayed. Betrayal is more than just hurt. It creates a sense of uncertainty. How can I trust someone who broke it the first time? What are the chances that they will not do it again? If I forgive my partner this time, what if they take this forgiveness for granted?

Infidelity can question the foundation of your relationship. You are angry and wondering if the relationship is worth saving or not. The good news, however, is that trust can be rebuilt if you are mentally, physically, and emotionally ready to forgive your partner and stay with them. The work involved isn't the same for both partners. The partner who betrayed will have to begin by taking full responsibility for their action and live up to the promises they make this time. The betrayed partner will have to ensure they don't keep bringing up the affair just to win arguments and make their partner feel unfairly judged. The reason I think the betrayed partner has to do more work is that they have to decide how they feel about being cheated. Do they think they can recover from something like this? Do they feel they won't feel bothered whenever their spouse talks to someone of the opposite gender? Can they heal and move on?

Unfortunately, there is no surefire way to rip off the pain like a bandage. Even the suggestions made later won't guarantee that your partner won't cheat on you in the future, or that your marriage will be a success moving on. But because you have decided to forgive your partner and work on this relationship, here's how things will look moving forward.

Keep communication lines open. Have an open and honest conversation about leaving the past behind, and moving forward as a couple. There should be clarity in your conversation. Don't hold anything back, especially if you are the betrayed partner. Ask questions that worry you, whether about the past or future. Talk about the changes you two expect in each other's behaviors and actions. Talk about how you plan to avoid any such situation in the future. Discuss these details before a new beginning. Talking honestly about what happened and why it happened will help you establish healthier boundaries for the future.

Second, don't take your relationship for granted. If you are the betrayed partner, you might begin to lose interest in the relationship. If you stayed back for kids, financial security, or some other reason than love, the chances of you feeling interested in making it work will be low. But don't be in it half-heartedly. Be as enthusiastic about your relationship as you were when you both started dating and fell in love. If you are in it for societal or family pressure, ask for more time to reconsider than be in it blindly. Let your wounds heal, and only if you picture yourself spending the rest of your life with your partner, stay. You won't be able to rebuild trust if you take your marriage for granted.

Don't forget the 3 As: appreciation, affection, and attention. Every partner in a romantic companionship seeks these three things from their partner. When any of these are lacking, cheating becomes easier. Now that you have begun the second chapter of your marriage, focus on an abundance of these three toward your partner. Center your efforts on showing affection, attending to your partner's needs, and appreciating their presence in your life. Don't wait for them to ask for it. Just offer whenever you can.

Re-initiate physical intimacy. This is possibly the most difficult, yet the most important step in rebuilding trust between partners. Sex demands an emotional connection. It requires that both partners are in the act equally. There shouldn't be any hesitation or disinterest. The betrayed partner may feel hurt and the betrayer might not want to initiate, fearing rejection. But don't underestimate the power of sex. Both of you should try to re-date yourself. Relive those days when you were most in love. Flirt with one another, dress up sexy and try some teasing. Make sex irresistible. Set the mood, engage in foreplay, bring flowers, cook something sweet, and try different positions and toys. You can always take baby steps, but keep the momentum going. Keep trying until you both feel comfortable with each other.

Promise to live up to what you commit. If you are the betrayer, you have already broken your partner's trust. Now is the time for you to step up your game and commit to your promises 100%. This will be a long-term investment this time, so be patient. Your partner won't be swayed away by just sweet talk like before. This time, you will have to fulfill every promise you make, and keep your word.

As for the betrayed, be open and welcoming of what your partner is offering. Value your partner's contribution, and praise their effort.

Make new rules. Since you are starting afresh, it makes sense that you set new expectations and rules in your messages. This is to improve communication and connection between you two. For example, you can make a rule between yourselves to keep each other in the loop about your day's activities. Schedule calls between lunch hours and in the evening before coming home. Schedule date nights every other week or monthly. Set healthy boundaries, divide chores, commit to meeting each other's friends and colleagues, talk about managing finances, etc.

I also like the idea of setting non-negotiable marriage meetings every week. This is to strengthen the bond between you two, and to stay informed about what's happening in your separate lives. If you have kids, it will be an ideal time to discuss something important related to them. If you are worried about how your spouse manages finances, you can talk about it as well, or you can communicate any issues that you previously kept to yourself, etc.

Plan, plan, and then plan some more. As the one betrayed, your worse fear right now is of it happening in the future. You don't know if your poor heart will make it. Therefore, work together and develop a plan to prevent it from happening again. Talk about any insecurities or worries you have that you are still afraid to voice. Talk about the reasons that created mistrust in the first place. Was it a lack of sexual or emotional intimacy? Was it a long-distance relationship and the absence of your partner from your daily life? Whichever was the case, develop a plan to avoid further breaches of trust. Make it a habit to call or text each other every time you feel unsure about something. Find time to spend together. Explore new interests and hobbies. Make future plans and create rituals of connection.

As you know, prevention is better than cure. I want to talk more about this plan of preventing further breaches of trust. Let that be the last but most important thing about this book: how to prevent your partner from cheating on you again.

NEVER AGAIN — PREVENTING AN AFFAIR FROM RECURRING

Forget enough to get over it. Remember enough so it doesn't happen again.

– Unknown

IF YOU HAVE BEEN betrayed once in your marriage by the person you trusted the most, the fear of it happening again is inevitable. You may think that things have improved and your relationship is stronger than ever, but there is still a doubt in the back of your head that keeps you alert. Why are they spending so much time in the bathroom? Why are they always on their phone? Who is calling them after work hours? You are constantly worried that the trauma you left behind will find you again.

Your fears aren't wrong. What you feel is quite normal, especially if the affair wasn't a long time ago. However, there are things you can do to ensure that it doesn't happen again. Since cheating has a direct effect on everyone in the family and not just you, it makes sense that you explore ideas that prevent your partner from cheating on you again.

Here's what comes recommended.

Have explicit arguments. Don't assume things on your own. Talk them through. Discuss anything and everything with your partner. Don't remain in the dark about anything because when you do, your thoughts play a twisted game and get you thinking all the wrong things. So keep arguing and letting things out. If you keep them in for long, they will corrode your mind.

Define what counts as cheating. Set new rules for what constitutes cheating. Do you feel upset when your partner likes pictures of other men and women on Instagram? Do you feel left out because your partner rarely shares anything personal with you? Do you think your partner needs to have some boundaries around their colleagues? Be on the same page about this to prevent any misunderstandings later.

Fulfill your own and your partner's emotional and physical needs. If they feel satisfied and fulfilled, they won't have any reason to look elsewhere. Be vocal about your needs and wants, and ask them to be vocal about theirs. Communicate with each other honestly; if they have needs you can't meet, find a compromise. As long as things are clearly communicated, the chances of another case of infidelity will be reduced.

Try also, though, not to get jealous when you sense your partner's attention drifting away. Instead, look for ways to win it back. Being critical and judging will only push them further away. Do things to woo them over. Give them reasons to love you and you alone.

Prevent cheating from recurring again by limiting your partner's opportunities. Are they traveling with a coworker? Are they going to places where drinking happens? Do they have independent social circles? Pay extra attention to instances that create an opportunity for cheating. If possible, request to travel together. If going with your partner isn't an option, send care packages to where they are to stay in their mind and heart. When out with friends for a drink, ask your partner to keep texting you so they don't consume too much, stay in touch when they are with their friends, and make it a rule to call when staying out late, so you don't worry or overthink.

Discuss sex like you discuss any other topic. Be open about trying new things in the bedroom. Share your fantasies and fetishes, and try what you feel comfortable with. Sometimes, partners need more than just casual sex. They need foreplay and some kinkiness. If you won't keep your partner entertained and enthusiastic about what's coming into the bedroom, their interest will drift away.

Don't be too controlling of their actions. Just because they strayed away once doesn't mean they will do it again. Give your partner some room to be themselves. Don't demand explanations the minute they enter the door. Don't threaten to leave, or remind them of their previous affair to punish them. However, at the same time, don't be too accommodating, thinking that if you give them time and space, they will feel grateful. Don't let them walk all over you. If they are staying late at the office just to enjoy some time with their colleagues, but do not have time for you when they come home, don't accommodate this carelessness.

CONCLUSION

The extent to which two people in a relationship can bring up and resolve issues is a critical marker of the soundness of a relationship.

– Henry Cloud

MARRIAGE REQUIRES SOME MORE work. It has many ups and downs, adventures, and memories that you make with the person you love. But that same person sometimes ends up hurting you in the cruelest of ways. They do what many call the "undoable" with someone other than their partner. They give away what was solely for their significant other to someone who isn't that: their love, time, and affection.

And it hurts. You know it because you have been through it. You are reading this book because you are at a crossroads. You have decided to stay and give your partner another chance, but are still unsure if it will work this time around or not.

For any marriage to be successful, both partners must tend to their garden equally. We often assume that we know our partners inside out. But people change. Circumstances change. We get lazy about showing love and care. We put our relationship in the backseat. Therefore, you must at all times be open and communicative about your needs and feelings. Effective communication between partners is what keeps them together. Don't think that your worries will bother your partner. Be vulnerable together. Don't wait for them to guess.

As important as communication is to any successful relationship, so is listening. Don't just talk to your partner, but also listen to what they have to say in return. With all that's going on in our lives, it is unsurprising that we forget to listen. We respond thoughtlessly, not taking our partner's feelings and emotions into consideration. To prevent that from happening, spend some quality time together. Do things you enjoy doing, be it in the bedroom or outside. Make your relationship a priority by all means. Don't hold back.

If you have decided to stay and forgive your partner, ensure that you grow together. Support each other and give each other a chance to prove your worth. As long as you support each other and can count on each other for advice and feedback, you can conquer the world.

So, what I have been trying to explain in this guide is that compassion and kindness between partners are what foster love. Let bygones be bygones. Move on with the same zest and passion you had for your partner at the beginning of the marriage.

This is now the second chapter of your marriage. Make sure not to repeat the mistakes you two made in the first.

COULD YOU HELP

THANK YOU SO MUCH for reading my book and for making it all the way to the end!

I would like to ask you for a small favor. Would you consider sharing your thoughts about my book and post a review on the Amazon platform? Your support means the world to me, as it will help my book gain visibility and attract a wider audience.

Thank you so much for your time and I truly appreciate it!

GIFT FOR YOU

SOMETHING'S OFF ABOUT YOUR partner, but you don't know what. Suddenly, they are spending hours in the washroom with their phone, making excuses about their boss keeping them after work hours, sneaking out of the room to take calls late at night, and being uninterested in having sex. Are they conscious about the way they look, upgrading their wardrobe, and hitting the gym? But this isn't like them!

What changed?

Deep down you know... you just don't want to admit it yet.

A cheating partner reveals more through their behavior and actions than through their words. But how to confirm the suspicions, and confront them with evidence?

How to make that confrontation a pivotal point in your relationship where you ask yourself if you want to continue living with the same person? Or leave and move on?

In *How to Discover and Confront Infidelity in Your Relationship*, the author unravels the many warning signs a cheating spouse/partner displays, and also shows how to confirm those doubts. With concrete evidence, let's prepare to have a sensible confrontation, and determine the reasons why your partner cheated...

(Download it for free at www.littlebookhut.com)

ALSO BY ELLIE FLORES

Start Loving Again: How to Resolve All Trust Issues, Build Trust in Relationship and Create a Loving Relationship You Deserve (ISBN:978-1955847049)

Connecting Love Question Book for Couple: 100 Fun and Thought-Provoking Questions to Strengthen Your Relationship and Rekindle Your Emotional Intimacy (ISBN:978-1955847032)

Printed in Great Britain
by Amazon